EVERYTHING SPORTS

EVERYTHING LACROSSE

SEAN SHAPIRO

SportsZone
An Imprint of Abdo Publishing
abdobooks.com

abdobooks.com

Published by Abdo Publishing, a division of ABDO, PO Box 398166, Minneapolis, Minnesota 55439.

Printed in the United States of America, North Mankato, Minnesota.
052024
092024

THIS BOOK CONTAINS
RECYCLED MATERIALS

Cover Photos: Mitchell Leff/Getty Images Sport/Getty Images (foreground); Shutterstock Images (background)
Interior Photos: MPI/Archive Photos/Getty Images, 4–5; Hulton Archive/Getty Images, 7; Tom Beary/Sportsfile/Getty Images, 9; David John Griffin/Icon Sportswire/Getty Images, 10–11; Steve Russell/Toronto Star/Getty Images, 12; Ryan Hunt/Getty Images Sport/Getty Images, 14–15; Larry French/NCAA Photos/Getty Images, 16–17, 20–21, 50–51; Grant Halverson/NCAA Photos/Getty Images, 18–19, 27; Hulton-Deutsch Collection/Corbis Historical/Getty Images, 22–23; Ben McCanna/Portland Press Herald/Getty Images, 25; Mike Caudill/The Washington Post/Getty Images, 28; Greg Fiume/NCAA Photos/Getty Images, 29, 36–37; Peyton Williams/Getty Images Sport/Getty Images, 31; Mitchell Leff/Getty Images Sport/Getty Images, 32–33; Angela Rowlings/Media News Group/Boston Herald/Getty Images, 34; Mike Moore/WireImage/Getty Images, 38–39; Justin Tafoya/Getty Images for NLL/Getty Images Sport/Getty Images, 41, 52–53; JHU Sheridan Libraries/Gado/Archive Photos/Getty Images, 43; Mark Evans/Getty Images for the AOC/Getty Images Sport/Getty Images, 44–45; Leon Halip/WireImage/Getty Images, 47; Michael Steele/Getty Images Sport/Getty Images, 48; Jim Rogash/Getty Images Sport/Getty Images, 54–55; Patrick Smith/Getty Images Sport/Getty Images, 57; George Rinhart/Corbis Historical/Getty Images, 59; Shutterstock Images, 60

Editor: Charlie Beattie
Series Designer: Karli Kruse

Library of Congress Control Number: 2023949394
Publisher's Cataloging-in-Publication Data
Names: Shapiro, Sean, author.
Title: Everything lacrosse / by Sean Shapiro
Description: Minneapolis, Minnesota: Abdo Publishing, 2025 | Series: Everything sports | Includes online resources and index.
Identifiers: ISBN 9781098293598 (lib. bdg.) | ISBN 9798384912866 (ebook)
Subjects: LCSH: Lacrosse--Juvenile literature. | Lacrosse players--Juvenile literature. | Lacrosse--Coaching--Juvenile literature. | Lacrosse--Rules--Juvenile literature. | Sports teams--Juvenile literature. | Sports--Juvenile literature.
Classification: DDC 796.347--dc23

TABLE OF CONTENTS

CHAPTER ONE

WHAT IS LACROSSE?

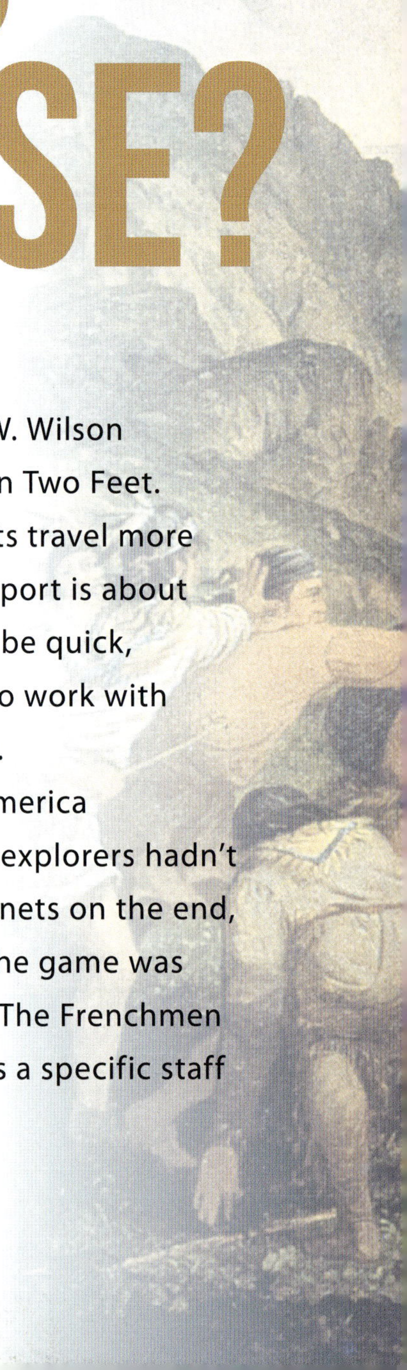

In 1921, a journalist from Baltimore named W. Wilson Wingate called lacrosse the Fastest Game on Two Feet. That is possibly still true. Today, lacrosse shots travel more than 100 miles per hour (161 km/h). But the sport is about more than just speed. Lacrosse players must be quick, agile, and tough. They also need to be able to work with teammates and carry out complex strategies.

In the 1600s, French explorers in North America witnessed native people playing a game the explorers hadn't seen before. Using wooden sticks fixed with nets on the end, the indigenous players were tossing a ball. The game was fast-paced, exciting, and sometimes violent. The Frenchmen thought the stick looked like a crozier. That is a specific staff

Lacrosse is a sacred sport to many indigenous nations in the United States and Canada.

that a bishop carries. The French word for it is *crosse*. That is how the sport of lacrosse got its modern name.

The game was a huge part of the culture for several indigenous nations. Each nation played with different rules and customs. The sport was viewed as both a way to solve problems and to prepare young men for battle. Some nations played games that took three days. Others played on fields that stretched for miles. The nations of the Haudenosaunee Confederacy live in what is now New York and Ontario, Canada. In the 1600s, these nations were known as the Iroquois. They played a version that looks like modern sport. It had 12 to 15 players per side and set field dimensions. The Haudenosaunee called their game both baggataway and tewaraathon.

The sport's rules were not written down until 1867. That's when George Beers, a member of the Montreal Lacrosse Club, decided to set standards for the game he loved. Beers, who was also a dentist, became known as the Father of Lacrosse. Beers limited each team to 12 players on the field. He adapted the ball to the hard rubber model players still use today. Beers also improved sticks to make it easier to both throw and catch. Beers staged many lacrosse exhibitions to spread the popularity of the game. He even played in front of England's Queen Victoria.

A member of the Canadian military carries a set of lacrosse sticks to a game on a base in England during World War II (1939–1945).

From there, lacrosse began to grow slowly in England as well as North America. American college students first started playing the sport in the 1870s. Women's lacrosse started to take off in the 1920s. Today, the sport is rapidly growing. The National Federation of State High School Associations reported more than 209,000 players in the 2022–23 school year. That was up more than 85,000 participants since the 2006–07 school year.

The game is still sacred to the indigenous people who created it. Members of the Onondaga Nation gift miniature lacrosse sticks to newborns. These are known as "crib sticks." The Haudenosaunee Nationals are made up of indigenous Americans and members of Canada's First Nations. The team's mission is to carry on the idea that lacrosse is a spiritual game for the continent's native people.

CANADA'S NATIONAL GAME

In 1967, Canada's prime minister, Lester B. Pearson, proposed a law that would name ice hockey and lacrosse as the country's dual national sports. Pearson's bill didn't pass. But in 1994, Canada passed the National Sports of Canada Act. Today, ice hockey is the country's official winter sport. Lacrosse is Canada's national summer sport.

The Haudenosaunee Nationals were formed in 1983. The team regularly competes in world championships.

CHAPTER TWO

TAKING THE FIELD

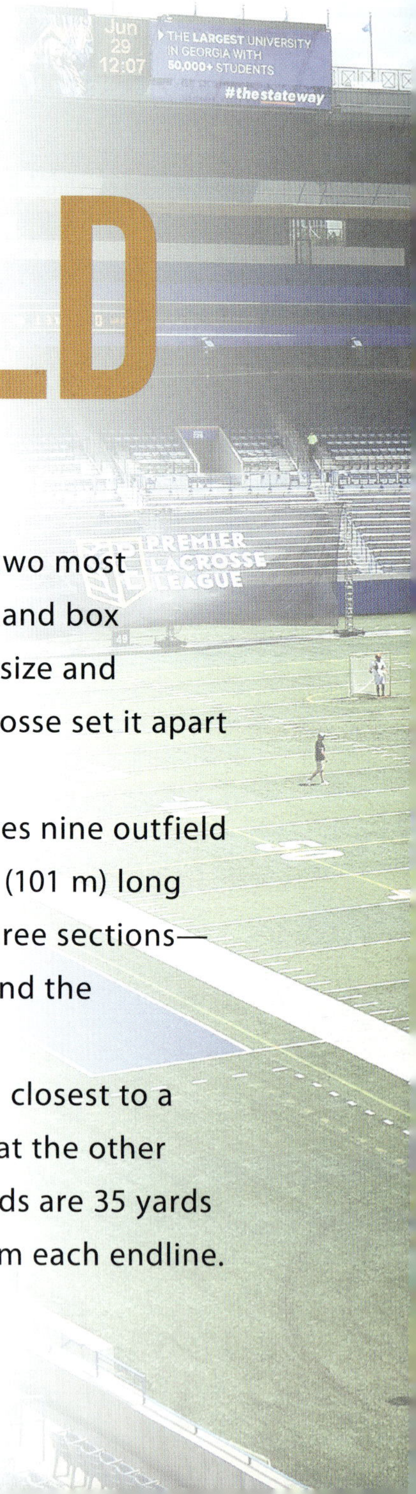

There are many variations of lacrosse. The two most common men's versions are field lacrosse and box lacrosse. Each has different rules about field size and number of players. The rules of women's lacrosse set it apart from both men's versions.

Field lacrosse is played outdoors. It features nine outfield players and one goalie. The field is 110 yards (101 m) long and 60 yards (55 m) wide. It is divided into three sections—the defensive area, the midfield/wing area, and the attacking area.

The defensive area is the third of the field closest to a team's defensive goal. The attacking third is at the other end of the field. Both attacking/defensive ends are 35 yards (32 m) long. The goals are 15 yards (14 m) from each endline.

Football and soccer fields are often used for field lacrosse.

Despite using smaller goals, professional box lacrosse games average about 25 goals per contest.

Each sits inside a circular crease. Field lacrosse goals for both men and women are six feet (1.8 m) by six feet.

The 40-yard (37-m) section in the middle is known both as the midfield and the wing area. Faceoffs take place there. That section also includes both teams' benches on the sideline. When players substitute, they must enter and exit the field in the midfield area. Because players can change during the action, substituting becomes a tricky piece of strategy.

Box lacrosse arose in the 1920s and 1930s. It is played indoors with boards lining the edges of the field. Box lacrosse fields are often set up in hockey rinks, and the games look very similar. Like hockey, box lacrosse teams are made up of five outfield players, called runners, and one goalie. Box lacrosse nets are also smaller. The box lacrosse net is four feet (1.2 m) high and four feet wide.

Women's lacrosse is played with 11 outfield players and one goalie. The field does not have a standard size. It can be anywhere from 60 to 70 yards (55–64 m) wide and 110 to 140 yards (101–128 m) long. As in the men's game, the field is divided into defensive, offensive, and midfield zones. The midfield zone is separated from the offensive and defensive areas by a mark known as the restraining line.

LACROSSE SIXES

Lacrosse sixes is the newest version of the sport. It was created in 2021. The game is played outdoors but features only five players per team plus a goalie. It is played on a 77-yard (70-meter) field that is 39 yards (36 m) wide. Sixes was created to make a faster-paced version of traditional field lacrosse. It will be featured in the 2028 Olympic Games.

The women's goal crease is much larger than the men's version. It is nine feet (8 m) across. The men's crease is only three feet (0.9 m) across. Additionally, the women's crease is attached to two other lines. One is the eight-meter (26-foot) arc. The other is the 12-meter (39-foot) fan. Both lines are used to help determine certain fouls.

Equipment for the three versions is also different. Men's lacrosse players in both field and box lacrosse wear protective helmets, shoulder pads, and gloves. The main difference between the two is what goaltenders wear. Field lacrosse goalies use a stick with a larger pocket. They do not wear any other special equipment. Box lacrosse goalies wear full padding, including on their legs. Because women's games do not allow body contact, players do not have to wear helmets, gloves, or shoulder pads. The only safety equipment women have to wear is a protective set of eye goggles.

In the United States, women's players were not required to wear eye protection until 2005.

CHAPTER THREE

POSITIONS AND ROLES

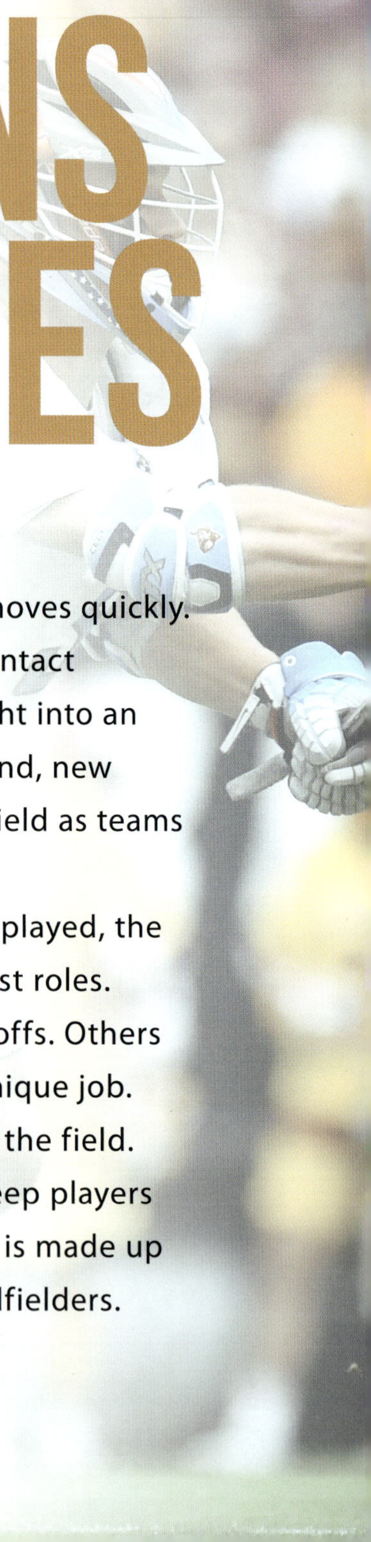

A lacrosse game can look like chaos. The ball moves quickly. The players weave around one another. In contact versions of the sport, sometimes they weave right into an opponent. And as the play moves from end to end, new players are constantly shuttling on and off the field as teams look for the right matchups.

No matter which version of lacrosse is being played, the positions on the field are a collection of specialist roles. Some players come on the field just to win faceoffs. Others only play defense. Goaltenders always have a unique job.

Other players can cover only certain areas of the field. In women's lacrosse, the two restraining lines keep players within the zones they are allowed in. Each team is made up of three defenders, three attackers, and five midfielders.

Luke Nestor of Salisbury University tries to keep the ball away from a defender during the 2023 NCAA Division III championship game.

Speed and finesse are key skills for women's lacrosse players.

While the midfielders can cover the entire field, the defenders and attackers have to stay in certain areas. Attacking players cannot go back behind the restraining line on the attacking half of the field. Defenders can't advance beyond the restraining line that sits 30 yards from their own goal.

In men's field lacrosse, each team has three attackers, three midfielders, and three defensemen. And while they can all move anywhere on the field, there are limits. Each team must have three defenders and a goalie on the defensive half of the field at all times. If a defender or goalie makes a run up field, a midfielder or forward has to stay back to make up for it.

While all women's players use a standard stick, defenders in the men's game use longer poles. This helps them break up plays and stick check opponents from farther away. However, long sticks are harder to shoot with.

THE LSM

In men's field lacrosse, a team will often sub in a fourth player using a long stick when they are transitioning to defense. This is known as the Long-Stick Midfielder, or LSM. LSMs don't just give a team an extra defensive stick when needed. They are often skilled midfielders who can carry the ball and start attacks. LSMs are often used in faceoff situations as well. Having the extra long pole on the field can help a team gain possession.

The shaft of an attacker's stick in men's lacrosse is usually 30 inches (76 cm) long, while a defender's stick is 60 inches (152 cm).

That's why defenders will rarely shoot when they venture up the field. Often, they will look to gain the attack zone and pass the ball off to a short stick as soon as possible.

In box lacrosse, players are divided up into forwards, defenders, transition players, and goaltenders. Transition players are the keys to any team. They need to be able to play both offense and defense well. It is their job to get the ball quickly from defense to attack. That way a team can catch its opponents on a fast break and score before the defense can set up.

CHAPTER FOUR

WOMEN'S LACROSSE

Louisa Lumsden was the headmistress at the St. Leonard's School in Scotland in the late 1800s. On a trip to Canada, she saw lacrosse being played. Lumsden described the game as "beautiful and graceful." She decided to introduce the sport at her school. In 1890, the first women's lacrosse team was formed at St. Leonard's.

Nearly two decades later, Rosabelle Sinclair was a student at St. Leonard's. She played on the school's team. Sinclair moved to Baltimore later in life and became a teacher. In 1926 she worked at Bryn Mawr School. There, Sinclair founded the first US-based girls lacrosse team. Soon, women's lacrosse spread in the region. In 1931, the US Women's Lacrosse Association was formed.

Players for the United States and England battle for a ball during a game in the early 1950s.

The sport grew slowly. In 1971, fewer than 500 girls played high school lacrosse in the United States. But a decade later, there were enough players internationally to hold a world championship. The United States beat Australia in the first championship game in 1982. In 2022, the Americans won their ninth title in 11 tournaments. Australia had won the other two. But it wasn't until the 2000s that women's lacrosse exploded. Between 2003 and 2008, the number of Division I women's teams grew by 97 percent.

ROSABELLE SINCLAIR

The National Lacrosse Hall of Fame inducted its first members in 1957. For 35 years, all the inductees were men. That changed in 1992 when Rosabelle Sinclair was admitted as the first female member. In addition, the field at Bryn Mawr School in Baltimore is named after Sinclair.

One of the biggest changes from the men's game to the women's game is the eight-meter shot. When a major foul is committed inside the eight-meter arc in the women's game, every player has to clear out. They have to stand outside the arc until the referee blows the whistle. Then, the player who was fouled gets a free shot. She has the option to shoot right away or move in on the goaltender. But if she does, the defenders then have a chance to pursue and break

A high school player in Maine fires an eight-meter shot.

up the play. Taking advantage of eight-meter chances is one of the major strategies at work in the women's game.

CHAPTER FIVE

THE FACEOFF

The faceoff is a play that can sway the course of a game. Faceoffs are often referred to as draws or "the battle at the X." They occur at the center of the field to start each quarter and after a goal is scored.

In women's lacrosse, a player from each team lines up facing each other in the faceoff circle. They hold their sticks parallel to the ground at waist height. The referee places the ball between their sticks. When the whistle is blown, the players use their sticks to push the ball above their heads. Then they fight for control.

Faceoffs look a bit different in the men's game. Two players crouch across from each other, each with one knee on the ground. They hold their sticks on the ground, parallel to the center line. The official places the ball on the center line between them. Their possession battles can look a little like wrestling matches as the two players fight to jar the ball free.

Jane Earley, *left*, of Middlebury prepares for a faceoff against Kathryn Delaney of Tufts during a 2023 game.

By consistently winning faceoffs, a lacrosse team can control the ball for most of the game.

Mastering the art of faceoffs takes a blend of speed, skill, and anticipation. Players must have swift reflexes to react to the referee's whistle. Their skill lies not only in winning control. They also try to direct the ball to their teammates at the best spots to start a possession.

Possession is key in lacrosse. Winning a faceoff creates an opportunity to launch an instant offensive attack. Teams can control the game's pace by keeping possession. Losing a faceoff can place the defensive team under pressure.

Some players are known as faceoff specialists. They focus primarily on faceoffs and quick transitions. These athletes use a variety of methods to beat their opponents to the ball. The winner of a faceoff can be decided by the slightest adjustments in technique and timing. Players must anticipate

In women's lacrosse, teammates cannot move into the draw circle until the ball is in the air.

the opponent's movements and react quickly to win possession. Every second counts.

Good coaches pay close attention to faceoffs. They select the best player for the job and work on tactics to make the most of each possession. A well-executed faceoff strategy can be a game-changer, particularly in a close contest. That was never truer than in the 2010 men's national championship game. Duke and Notre Dame went to overtime tied 5–5. CJ Costabile, an LSM for Duke, took the opening faceoff. He won it cleanly, swept the ball past his opponent and took off down the field. Costabile charged forward and fired the winning goal for the Blue Devils. In five seconds, Duke went from battling for possession to winning the national championship.

TREVOR BAPTISTE

Trevor Baptiste was one of the greatest faceoff specialists ever. He played college lacrosse for the University of Denver from 2015 to 2018. When he graduated, Baptiste held the National Collegiate Athletic Association (NCAA) career records of 1,158 faceoff wins and a 71.4 winning percentage. As a freshman, Baptiste helped the Pioneers win their first national title.

CJ Costabile won a team-high 97 faceoffs for Duke in 2010. He also won six out of 10 in the championship game against Notre Dame.

CHAPTER SIX

COLLEGE LACROSSE

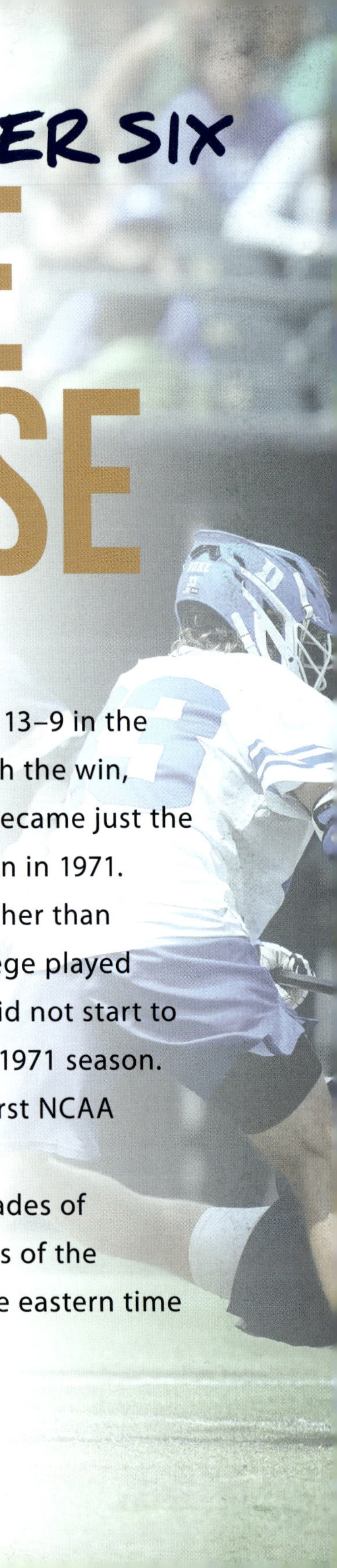

On May 29, 2023, Notre Dame defeated Duke 13–9 in the men's Division I lacrosse championship. With the win, the Fighting Irish joined an elite group. They became just the 12th team to win the tournament since it began in 1971.

Men's college lacrosse goes back much further than that. New York University and Manhattan College played the first college game in 1877. But the NCAA did not start to recognize lacrosse as a varsity sport until that 1971 season. That year, Cornell beat Maryland 12–6 in the first NCAA championship game.

East Coast schools dominated the first decades of lacrosse. In fact, very few schools in other parts of the country even had teams. No school outside the eastern time

Chris Kavanagh (50) of Notre Dame scores one of his two goals in the 2023 men's national championship.

Syracuse and Johns Hopkins have played each other in the men's national championship game five times.

zone won a men's title before 2015. That year, the Denver Pioneers knocked off Maryland 10–5.

The men's game has seen several dynasties. Johns Hopkins University won seven titles between 1974 and 1987.

The Blue Jays have nine titles overall. Syracuse University broke that record in 2009 by winning its 10th championship. The Orange did it in dramatic fashion. They tied Cornell with 4.5 seconds left in regulation. Syracuse then won the game 10–9 in overtime.

However, no school has been as dominant in lacrosse as the Maryland women's team. The NCAA started a women's tournament in 1982. The Terrapins won their first title in 1986. They crushed their competition in the late 1990s. Between 1995 and 2001, Maryland won seven straight. In 2019, the Terrapins claimed their record 14th championship with a 12–10 win over Boston College.

Over the decades, fan support for lacrosse has exploded. The first men's title game was played in front of

LOWER DIVISION POWERS

The NCAA started staging a Division II men's tournament in 1974. The Division III tournament started in 1980. Hobart College in New York won the first 12 Division III titles. The Statesmen added a 13th in 1993. Salisbury University matched that total in 2023. The women's Division III tournament began in 1985. The College of New Jersey won the first tournament. By 2006, the Lions had added 11 more titles. Since the Division II women's tournament debuted in 2001, the Adelphi University Panthers have won a record nine championships.

fewer than 6,000 fans at Hofstra Stadium in Hempstead, New York. The 2023 championship game was played at Lincoln Financial Field in Philadelphia. It is the home stadium of pro football's Eagles. The crowd that watched Notre Dame and Duke totaled 30,462 fans. But even that was well short of the overall record. In 2008, 48,970 fans packed Gillette Stadium in Foxborough, Massachusetts, to watch Syracuse defeat Johns Hopkins 13–10.

The Maryland Terrapins celebrate their 12–10 victory over Boston College in the 2019 women's national championship game.

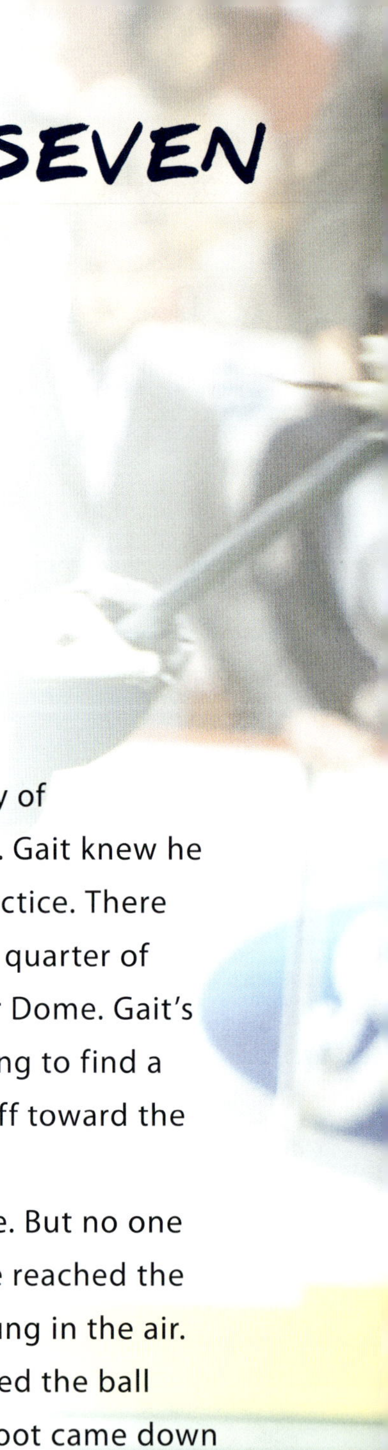

CHAPTER SEVEN
TAKING FLIGHT

Gary Gait was standing behind the University of Pennsylvania net when he saw his opening. Gait knew he could attempt a move he had tried only in practice. There were just over nine minutes left in the second quarter of the 1988 NCAA semifinals at Syracuse's Carrier Dome. Gait's Syracuse University was trailing Penn 2–1. Trying to find a way through the Quakers defense, Gait took off toward the back of the net.

Gait knew he couldn't set foot in the crease. But no one had ever told him he couldn't go over it. As he reached the back of the crease, Gait leaped upward and hung in the air. He then reached over the crossbar and slammed the ball downward into the net. By the time his right foot came down in the crease, Gait had tied the game.

Gary Gait, seen here playing for the Colorado Mammoth of the National Lacrosse League, was a standout college player at Syracuse University.

No one had ever tried Gait's move in a game. And no one who was there was sure the play was even legal. As almost 12,000 fans watched on, the officials debated. Finally, they decided that since Gait didn't have a foot on the ground in the crease when he scored, the goal counted.

GAIT'S CAREER

Gary Gait's contributions to lacrosse didn't stop with his famous play. He eventually played 18 years in the National Lacrosse League (NLL). He retired with 1,165 points. Gait also played for Canada in five world championship tournaments. His last came in 2006. Gait scored four goals in the final to help Canada beat the United States 15–10. It was Canada's first world title since 1978. Gait and his twin brother, Paul, were both superstars of the sport. They are credited with helping grow the game during the 1990s and 2000s.

Syracuse was trailing 4–3 in the third quarter when Gait pulled off the move again. Syracuse went on to win the game 11–10. The Orange then defeated Cornell 13–8 to win the national title.

Gait was the top scorer in that year's tournament with 18 goals. But it was the two he scored against Penn that shook the lacrosse world. His signature move eventually came to be known as the Air Gait. After the game, the debate went on as to whether or not the play should be allowed. Air Gait was eventually banned from the sport. However, the ban didn't last long.

Ian MacKay of the Buffalo Bandits tries an Air Gait play in the 2023 NLL championship series against the Colorado Mammoth.

The move was eventually reinstated in various professional leagues and NCAA play.

Even despite the bans, Gait had changed the sport. Just seeing Gait make his move changed how players looked at scoring. Many compared it to the first time someone dunked a basketball. “It kind of opened our minds up. . . . Hey, there’s another answer here,” said John Desko, who was an assistant for Syracuse in 1988. Soon, players began trying new tricks whenever they could. Today, many of the creative moves that offensive players make can trace their roots back to the Air Gait.

CHAPTER EIGHT

OLYMPIC LACROSSE

The third modern Olympic Games were held in 1904 in St. Louis. Not much about that event would be recognizable to people today. The Games were held as part of a World's Fair. The competitions took place over nearly five months. And of the 650 athletes, all but 107 were from the United States. One other twist? Those St. Louis Olympics included a men's lacrosse tournament.

Lacrosse has a distant and short Olympic history. The sport was included as a full medal event just two times, in 1904 and 1908. It returned as a demonstration event three other times between 1928 and 1948. However, no medals were awarded in those competitions.

The first Olympic lacrosse tournament featured three club teams. A team from Canada, the Winnipeg Shamrocks, beat a local team from St. Louis 8–2 to win the first gold medal.

Only two teams took part in the 1908 Olympics. A Canadian national team beat the hosts from Great Britain 14–10 to claim the gold medal.

Other international lacrosse tournaments formed over the years. These included the men's and women's World Championships. But for more than a century, lacrosse remained outside of the Olympics. Finally, that changed.

The United States was one of three countries to participate in the 1928 Olympic lacrosse tournament in Amsterdam, Netherlands. The others were Canada and Great Britain.

NATIVE TEAMS

In 1904, a Canadian club called the Mohawk Indians won the bronze medal. The team was made up of First Nations people from the Brantford, Ontario, region. Today's Haudenosaunee team is made up of Native Americans and Canadian First Nations members. Though the team plays in international lacrosse tournaments, as of 2023 the Haudenosaunee Confederacy was not recognized by the Olympics. Lacrosse officials said they were exploring ways to allow the Haudenosaunee to participate.

Lacrosse was one of five sports added to the 2028 Olympics in Los Angeles. In another twist, however, it was neither field nor box lacrosse that got the nod. Instead, the Olympics will feature a game called sixes. This fast-paced version of field lacrosse is played with smaller teams and on a smaller field. Each side has six active players, including the goalie. Games take just 32 minutes, and a shot clock ensures the action is always moving.

Lacrosse was added to the 2028 Olympic Games alongside baseball, cricket, flag football, softball, and squash.

CHAPTER NINE

AWARDS, HONORS, AND LEGENDS

In 2001, an award was created to honor the top collegiate players in both the men's and women's games. It was named the Tewaaraton Award. The name came from "tewaraathon," the name for lacrosse in the Mohawk language. The Mohawk nation is one of the members of the Haudenosaunee Confederacy. The award's name was meant as a tribute to lacrosse's indigenous roots.

In 2004, Syracuse attacker Michael Powell became the first player to win the award a second time. He had also won it in 2002. In 2007, Northwestern midfielder Kristen Kjellman won the award for the second consecutive time. She became the first back-to-back winner. Her teammate Hannah Nielsen followed up by matching that feat with the 2008 and

2009 awards. In 2016, Maryland midfielder Taylor Cummings became the sport's first three-time winner. Her run was part of a six-year stretch during which the women's award went to a Terrapins player every year.

Michael Powell had 150 goals and 157 assists in his four seasons at Syracuse.

Taylor Cummings, *left*, led Maryland to national championships in both 2014 and 2015. She won the Tewaaraton Award both years.

However, perhaps the most symbolic award winners came in 2014. That year, brothers Miles and Lyle Thompson of the University at Albany both won the men's award. That made them the first co-winners in Tewaaraton history.

However, that was only half of their story. Both Miles and Lyle are members of the Onondaga Nation. The Onondaga are part of the Haudenosaunee Confederacy. The Thompsons were the first indigenous winners of the award.

The United States Intercollegiate Lacrosse Association also recognizes the nation's top men's players with its own set of awards. The Enners Award is presented to the national player of the year. The Schmeisser Award honors the nation's top defenseman. The MacLaughlin Award goes to the midfielder of the year. The Turnbull Award honors the nation's top attacker. And the Kelly Award goes to the nation's top goalie.

JIM BROWN

Jim Brown became a legendary football player for the Cleveland Browns in the late 1950s and early 1960s. He retired as the National Football League's all-time leading rusher. But before that, Brown was a lacrosse superstar at Syracuse. The attacker was an All-American twice. Many consider him the greatest college lacrosse player ever. Brown spoke to an all-star group of professional players in 2019. In his speech, he called lacrosse his favorite sport.

Since the Tewaaraton Awards are so new, several great NCAA players never won one. Gary and Paul Gait were twin superstars for Syracuse in the late 1980s. Gary finished his career with 192 goals. Tim Nelson played for

North Carolina State and Syracuse between 1982 and 1985. His record of 221 career assists stood until Lyle Thompson broke it in 2015.

Jen Adams of Maryland was the first women's Tewaaraton winner in 2001. But had the award existed earlier she might have a few more. Adams set a new NCAA record with 148 points that season. The record she broke was her own. Adams had scored 136 points in 2000. She had also led the nation with 117 in 1999. Adams fell just short of the career record for goals when she finished with 267. Marsha Florio of Penn State scored 271 from 1982 to 1985. Her record did not last long, though. Gail Cummings of Temple racked up 289 goals from 1985 to 1988.

KELLY AMONTE HILLER

In women's lacrosse, Kelly Amonte Hiller's success is unmatched. Amonte Hiller helped Maryland win two national titles during her career as a player between 1993 and 1996. She left the school with a record 319 points. Amonte Hiller took over as the head coach of Northwestern in 2002. She quickly turned the Wildcats into a national powerhouse. In 2005, Northwestern became the first school outside the eastern time zone to win the national title. Amonte Hiller's Wildcats won their eighth national championship in 2023.

Jen Adams had five goals and five assists in the 2000 NCAA championship game to help Maryland beat Princeton University 16–8.

CHAPTER TEN

PROFESSIONAL LACROSSE

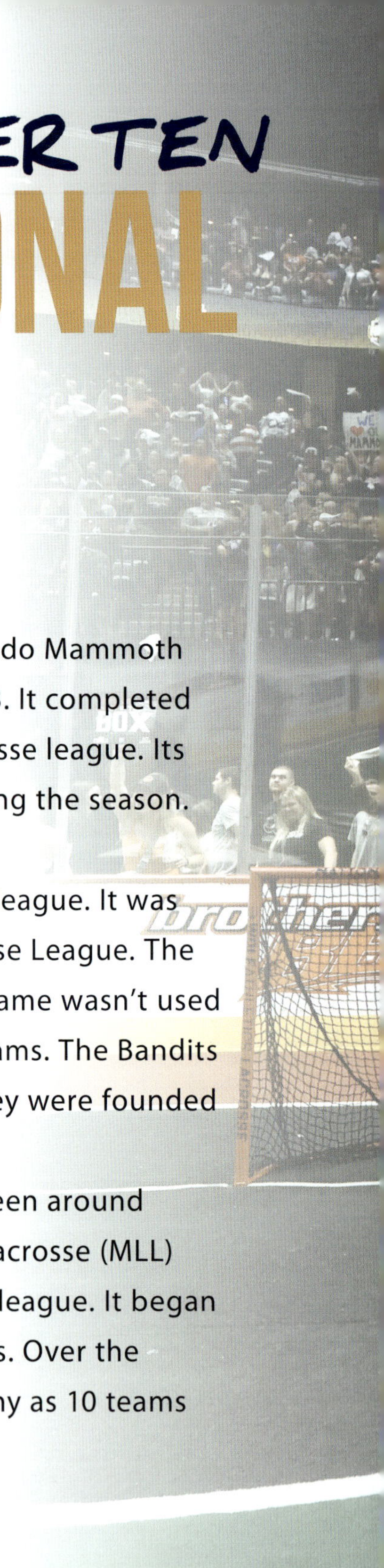

The Buffalo Bandits knocked off the Colorado Mammoth for the NLL championship on June 3, 2023. It completed a great season for the professional box lacrosse league. Its 15 teams drew more than 1 million fans during the season. That hadn't happened since 2007–08.

The NLL is the oldest active professional league. It was founded in 1986 as the Eagle Pro Box Lacrosse League. The league has changed names twice. The NLL name wasn't used until 1997. It has also gone through many teams. The Bandits are the longest running team in the NLL. They were founded in 1991.

Professional box lacrosse leagues have been around since the 1930s. But in 1999, Major League Lacrosse (MLL) was founded as a professional field lacrosse league. It began with six teams in the Northeast United States. Over the next decade, the league expanded to as many as 10 teams

John Lintz of the Colorado Mammoth salutes the team's fans after Game 2 of the NLL championship series in 2023.

JOHN TAVARES

The Buffalo Bandits were coached by John Tavares in 2022–23. Tavares has been a huge part of the league's history. He spent 24 years as a player for the Bandits before retiring in 2015. When he left, the Toronto native held the league record with 306 games played. He had also scored 815 goals and handed out 934 assists for 1,749 points. All three totals were the most in NLL history. He was the league's Most Valuable Player three times.

across the country before contracting again.

Since MLL played its games in the summer and NLL games were mostly in the winter and spring, many players appeared in both leagues. One of those players was Paul Rabil. But in 2018, Rabil left both the NLL and MLL to form his own league. The Premier Lacrosse League (PLL) was set up in a different way. Instead of teams traveling from their home cities, the entire league travels together. The teams play 10 weekends every season. Each weekend, the games take place in a different city. In 2020, MLL and the PLL merged, with one of the MLL teams joining Rabil's new league.

The PLL field is shorter than a normal field lacrosse setup. And the league has added a few wrinkles to the traditional rules. The main difference is the addition of the two-point goal. Any shot from outside the 15-meter line counts as a two-point shot.

Paul Rabil (99) scored 403 professional goals between the NLL, MLL, and PLL before retiring in 2022.

There was no women's professional lacrosse league until 2018. That year, the Women's Professional Lacrosse League debuted with five teams. But when the COVID-19 pandemic hit in 2020, the league was forced to shut down.

The next year, Athletes Unlimited launched a new league. Like the PLL on the men's side, Athletes Unlimited tried some different ideas. The season is only five weeks long. But each week, the teams change. The four players who performed the best the week before become the next week's captains. They get to pick their teammates for the next week. At the end of the season, there is no team champion. Individual players win the league. Former three-time Tewaaraton Award winner Taylor Cummings won the first season. Former University of North Carolina goalkeeper Taylor Moreno won the next two seasons.

Whether it is field lacrosse or indoor box lacrosse, players today have many more opportunities for professional careers than in years past. And all three professional leagues are growing their fan bases in-person and on television. It is just another way that lacrosse is one of the fastest growing sports in North America.

Goaltender Taylor Moreno won 70 games at the University of North Carolina before joining Athletes Unlimited in 2022.

CHAPTER ELEVEN

EQUIPMENT EVOLUTION

Lacrosse sticks have come a long way since members of the Haudenosaunee created the sport nearly 1,000 years ago. Early lacrosse sticks were usually carved from hickory wood. The nets of these sticks were made from animal hide or gut. Leather strings fastened everything together. Each stick was a deeply personal item to its owner. Haudenosaunee men were often buried with their sticks so they could play again as soon as they reach the afterlife.

The first plastic stick heads were created in the 1970s. Aluminum shafts debuted in the 1980s. So did nets that were made of synthetic mesh. Modern sticks are made of composite metals. They are not only much lighter than traditional sticks but also more durable.

Just as the rules are different for men's and women's lacrosse, the players in each game use slightly different sticks. The main difference is in the pocket. Men's stick pockets are much deeper, which allows players to control the ball much more easily. Because the women's game does not allow for body contact that could knock the ball free, the

Lacrosse sticks used in the early 1900s had triangular-shaped heads.

Though women's lacrosse balls often differ in color from the men's, all lacrosse balls are the same size and weight.

shallower pocket allows a defender the chance to knock the ball loose and force turnovers.

The ball itself has also changed. Early lacrosse balls were made from several different materials. Some were made from buckskin. Others were made from wood or even rocks. They weren't even always round.

Today's balls are made of what is known as vulcanized rubber. This means the rubber has been treated with chemicals to make it harder. It is the same process used on car tires. While men's and women's lacrosse balls are the same size, the main difference is the color. Traditionally, men's lacrosse leagues have used plain white balls. However, some leagues have started using yellow and orange balls that are easier to see. Women's lacrosse players use yellow balls.

ALF JACQUES

Alf Jacques, a member of the Onondaga Nation, died at the age of 74 in 2023. He left behind quite a legacy. Jacques had spent the previous 50 years making traditional wooden lacrosse sticks by hand. His father, Lou, had taught Alf the art when Alf was just 12 years old. By the time he died, it was estimated that Jacques had crafted around 80,000 sticks.

GLOSSARY

banned
Stopped something from happening for a period of time.

composite
Made of different elements.

crease
The area in front of a goal where the goalie plays.

dynasties
Teams that have extended periods of success, usually winning multiple championships in the process.

elite
The highest level.

exhibition
A game that doesn't count in the standings.

indigenous
Relating to cultural groups who have a longstanding connection to an area of land or country.

merged
Joined with another to create something new, such as a company, a team, or a league.

overtime
An extra period of play when the score is tied after regulation.

parallel
Side-by-side.

professional
A person who gets paid to perform.

reflexes
Actions that do not require conscious thought.

specialist
A person who concentrates on one activity.

MORE INFORMATION

Books

Flynn, Brendan. *Girls' Lacrosse*. Abdo, 2022.

Hill, Cade. *How to Play Lacrosse for Beginners*. 2023.

Stathes, Corbu. *Everything Football*, Abdo, 2025.

Online Resources

Booklinks
NONFICTION NETWORK
FREE! ONLINE NONFICTION RESOURCES

To learn more about lacrosse, please visit **abdobooklinks.com** or scan this QR code. These links are routinely monitored and updated to provide the most current information available.

INDEX

About the Author

Sean Shapiro is a freelance author and journalist living in Michigan. He and his wife, Christina, are the proud parents of Evangeline and Dean.